# About The Author

Jason Mizrachi is a seasoned sales professional with extensive experience in driving revenue growth and building successful sales teams for over 25+ years. With a track record of consistently exceeding targets, Jason has a deep understanding of the sales process and what it takes to close deals.  His sometimes unconventional style in how he prospects and presents has put him above the rest in his success for driving nontraditional revenue.  He has a passion for mentoring and coaching others to succeed, and has a talent for developing effective sales strategies tailored to individual businesses. With his expertise in sales, Jason has helped numerous companies achieve their revenue goals and unlock new opportunities for growth.

*"I cut my teeth growing up in my Dad's electronic store when I was just a little kid and learning how to sell...it's in me"!*

# Chapter 1: Introduction to Sales Mastery

To become a sales hero, it is also important to understand the sales process. The sales process typically consists of several stages, from identifying potential customers to closing the sale. These stages may vary depending on the product or service being sold, but the general process is as follows:

1. Prospecting: This is the stage where potential customers are identified. Salespeople may use a variety of methods to generate leads, including cold calling, networking, or social media.

2. Qualifying: Once potential customers have been identified, the next step is to determine if they are a good fit for the product or service being sold. This may involve asking questions to understand their needs, budget, and timeframe.

3. Presenting: Once a potential customer has been qualified, the salesperson presents the product or service to them. This may involve a demonstration, a proposal, or a sales pitch.

4. Handling objections: During the presentation, potential customers may have objections or concerns. Successful salespeople can handle these objections and address them in a way that reassures the customer and builds trust.

5. Closing: This is the final stage of the sales process, where the salesperson asks for the sale. This may involve negotiating the terms of the sale or overcoming any final objections.

6. Follow-up: After the sale has been made, it is important to follow up with the customer to ensure they are satisfied with the product or service. This can help to build long-term relationships and lead to repeat business.

Understanding the sales process is essential to achieving sales mastery. Each stage of the process requires different skills and techniques, and successful salespeople are able to navigate each stage effectively.

In addition to the sales process, successful salespeople also understand the importance of building relationships with potential customers. Building relationships involves establishing trust and demonstrating the value of the product or service being sold. It may involve following up with potential customers regularly, providing them with helpful information, or offering exceptional customer service.

Finally, successful salespeople understand the importance of setting goals and measuring their progress. This may involve setting sales targets, tracking sales metrics, or evaluating their performance on a regular basis. By setting goals and measuring their progress, salespeople can identify areas for improvement and make the necessary changes to achieve sales mastery.

In summary, to achieve sales mastery and become a sales hero, it is important to understand the sales process, build relationships with potential customers, and set goals and measure progress. By developing these skills and following the steps outlined in the following chapters, you can achieve success in sales and become a true sales hero.

## Chapter 2: Understanding Your Target Market

To become a sales hero, it is important to understand your target market. The target market refers to the specific group of people who are most likely to be interested in the product or service you are selling. Understanding your target market involves researching and analyzing their needs, desires, and behavior. By understanding your target market, you can tailor your sales approach to meet their needs, which can lead to increased sales and customer loyalty.

The first step in understanding your target market is to define it. Your target market may be based on factors such as age, gender, income, location, or interests. Defining your target market allows you to focus your sales efforts on the group of people who are most likely to buy your product or service.

Once you have defined your target market, the next step is to research and analyze their needs and behavior. This may involve gathering data from market research reports, conducting surveys or focus groups, or analyzing social media and website analytics. By understanding your target market's needs and behavior, you can tailor your sales approach to meet their specific needs.

Another important aspect of understanding your target market is understanding their pain points. Pain points refer to the specific problems or challenges your target market may be facing. By understanding your target market's pain points, you can position your product or service as the solution to their problems. This can help to build trust and establish a relationship with potential customers.

It is also important to understand your target market's buying behavior. This may involve understanding their decision-making process, the factors that influence their purchasing decisions, and their preferred purchasing channels. By understanding your target market's buying behavior, you can tailor your sales approach to meet their specific preferences and needs.

In addition to understanding your target market's needs and behavior, it's also important to stay up to date on industry trends and developments. This can help you to anticipate changes in your target market and adjust your sales approach accordingly. Staying up to date on industry trends may involve attending conferences, reading industry publications, or networking with other sales professionals.

Finally, understanding your target market requires ongoing research and analysis. Your target market may change over time, and it is important to stay up to date on any changes or developments. This may involve conducting regular surveys, analyzing sales metrics, or monitoring social media and website analytics.

In summary, understanding your target market is essential to achieving sales mastery. By defining your target market, researching and analyzing their needs and behavior, understanding their pain points and buying behavior, staying up to date on industry trends, and conducting ongoing research and analysis, you can tailor your sales approach to meet their specific needs and become a true sales hero.

## Chapter 3: Building a Sales Strategy

To become a sales hero, it is important to develop a sales strategy that aligns with your business goals and target market. A sales strategy outlines the specific steps you will take to achieve your sales objectives and build long-term relationships with customers. In this chapter, we will discuss the key components of a successful sales strategy.

1. Set clear and specific sales goals: To develop a successful sales strategy, it's important to set clear and specific sales goals. These goals should be aligned with your overall business objectives and target market. Setting goals allows you to track your progress, measure your success, and adjust your strategy as needed.

2. Identify your unique selling proposition: Your unique selling proposition (USP) is what sets your

product or service apart from the competition. Your USP should be clear, concise, and easy to communicate to potential customers. Identifying your USP allows you to differentiate yourself from the competition and demonstrate the value of your product or service to potential customers.

3. Develop a customer profile: A customer profile outlines the specific characteristics of your target market. This may include demographic information, buying behavior, and pain points. Developing a customer profile allows you to tailor your sales approach to meet the specific needs of your target market.

4. Identify sales channels: Sales channels refer to the specific methods you will use to sell your product or service. This may include online sales, in-person sales, or sales through third-party distributors. Identifying your sales channels allows you to focus your sales efforts and allocate resources effectively.

5. Develop a sales process: A sales process outlines the specific steps you will take to move potential customers through the sales funnel. This may include methods for generating leads, qualifying leads, presenting your product or service, handling

objections, and closing the sale. Developing a sales process allows you to standardize your sales approach and ensure consistency in your sales efforts.

6. Define metrics for success: To measure the success of your sales strategy, it is important to define specific metrics that align with your sales goals. These may include metrics such as revenue, customer acquisition cost, or conversion rate. Defining metrics for success allows you to track your progress and adjust your sales strategy as needed.

7. Allocate resources: To execute your sales strategy effectively, it's important to allocate resources such as time, personnel, and budget. Allocating resources allows you to prioritize your sales efforts and ensure that you have the necessary resources to achieve your sales goals.

In summary, developing a sales strategy is essential to achieving sales mastery. By setting clear and specific sales goals, identifying your unique selling proposition, developing a customer profile, identifying sales channels, developing a sales process, defining metrics for success, and allocating resources, you can tailor your sales approach to meet the specific needs of your target market and become a true sales hero.

## Chapter 4: Prospecting and Lead Generation

Prospecting and lead generation are the lifeblood of sales. Without a steady stream of potential customers, even the most skilled salesperson will struggle to meet their sales goals. In this chapter, we will explore some of the most effective techniques for prospecting and lead generation.

1. Start with your existing network: Your existing network can be a valuable source of leads. Reach out to past customers, friends, family, and colleagues to see if they or anyone they know might be interested in your product or service. You can also leverage your social media presence to promote your business and attract potential customers.

2. Utilize referrals: Referrals are a powerful tool for generating new leads. Ask satisfied customers if they

know anyone who might be interested in your product or service and offer incentives for referrals. You can also consider partnering with other businesses to exchange referrals.

3. Attend networking events: Networking events provide an opportunity to meet potential customers and build relationships with other professionals in your industry. Look for events that are relevant to your target market and make a point to attend regularly. Be sure to bring business cards and be prepared to introduce yourself and your business.

4. Use online tools: Online tools such as social media, email marketing, and search engine optimization (SEO) can be powerful tools for lead generation. Develop a strong online presence by creating a professional website, engaging on social media, and building an email list. Utilize SEO techniques to ensure that your website appears high in search engine results for relevant keywords.

5. Cold outreach: Cold outreach involves reaching out to potential customers who have not expressed interest in your product or service. This can include cold calling, email outreach, or direct mail. While cold outreach can be effective, it is important to be

respectful of the potential customer's time and avoid being pushy or aggressive.

6. Attend trade shows and conferences: Trade shows and conferences provide an opportunity to connect with potential customers who are specifically interested in your industry or product. Be sure to bring marketing materials and be prepared to answer questions about your business.

7. Partner with influencers: Influencers are individuals or businesses with a large following on social media or in the industry. By partnering with influencers, you can reach a wider audience and attract potential customers who might not otherwise be aware of your business.

In summary, prospecting and lead generation are critical to sales success. By leveraging your existing network, utilizing referrals, attending networking events, using online tools, engaging in cold outreach, attending trade shows and conferences, and partnering with influencers, you can generate a steady stream of leads and build a strong sales pipeline. With a consistent flow of leads, you will be well on your way to becoming a sales hero.

# Chapter 5: Qualifying Leads and Opportunities

Once you have generated leads, it is time to qualify them to ensure that you are spending your time and resources on the most promising opportunities. Qualifying leads involves determining whether they have a need for your product or service, whether they have the authority to make purchasing decisions, whether they have the budget to afford your offering, and whether they are ready to make a decision in the near future.

Here are some techniques for qualifying leads and opportunities:

1. Ask the right questions: Ask open-ended questions that encourage potential customers to talk about their needs and pain points. Ask about their goals, their current challenges, and their decision-making process. This will help you determine whether they are a good fit for your offering and whether they are ready to move forward.

2. Do your research: Before engaging with a potential customer, do some research to learn more about their business, industry, and pain points. This will allow you to ask more targeted questions and demonstrate your expertise. It will also help you determine whether they are a good fit for your offering.

3. Identify decision-makers: Make sure that you are talking to the person who has the authority to make purchasing decisions. If you are talking to someone who is not the decision-maker, ask for an introduction to the decision-maker or for the best way to reach them.

4. Determine budget: Ask about their budget and whether they have the financial resources to afford your product or service. If they do not have the budget, it is better to move on to other leads that are more likely to result in a sale.

5. Determine timeline: Ask about their timeline for making a decision. If they are not ready to make a decision in the near future, it may be better to focus on other leads that are more likely to convert into sales.

6. Use a scoring system: Develop a scoring system that allows you to prioritize leads based on their likelihood to convert into sales. Assign points for factors such as budget, timeline, need, and decision-making authority, and use the scores to determine which leads to focus on first.

7. Be honest: If a lead does not meet your qualifications, be honest with them and move on. Do not waste your time and resources pursuing leads that are unlikely to result in a sale.

Qualifying leads and opportunities are critical to sales success. By asking the right questions, doing your research, identifying decision-makers, determining budget and timeline, using a scoring system, and being honest, you can focus your time and resources on the most promising opportunities and increase your chances of success. With a solid process for qualifying leads, you will be well on your way to becoming a sales hero.

## Chapter 6: Creating Winning Sales Presentations

A great sales presentation can make all the difference in closing a deal. A sales presentation is an opportunity to highlight your product or service and demonstrate how it can solve the prospect's pain points. Here are some tips to create a winning sales presentation.

1. Start with a hook: Begin your presentation with a hook that grabs the audience's attention. This could be a thought-provoking question, a surprising statistic, or a compelling story.

2. Identify pain points: Demonstrate that you understand the prospect's pain points and needs. Talk about the challenges they are facing and how your product or service can help them overcome those challenges.

3. Highlight benefits: Focus on the benefits of your product or service, rather than just the features. Discuss how your product or service can help the prospect save time, money, or increase productivity.

4. Use visuals: Use visuals such as images, graphs, and videos to make your presentation more engaging and

memorable. A picture is worth a thousand words, and visuals can help illustrate your points more effectively.

5. Tell a story: Use storytelling to make your presentation more memorable. Create a narrative that ties together the pain points, the benefits of your product or service, and how it can make a positive impact on the prospect's business.

6. Use social proof: Use social proof, such as customer testimonials and case studies, to demonstrate how your product or service has helped others in similar situations. This can help build credibility and trust with the prospect.

7. Provide a call to action: End your presentation with a clear call to action. This could be to schedule a follow-up meeting, to sign up for a trial, or to make a purchase. Make it easy for the prospect to take the next step.

8. Practice, practice, practice: Practice your presentation until you feel comfortable with the material. This will help you feel more confident and natural during the actual presentation.

9. Customize for the prospect: Customize your presentation for the specific prospect you are

presenting to. Research their business, industry, and tailor your presentation to their specific pain points and needs.

10. Follow up: After the presentation, follow up with the prospect to answer any additional questions and to keep the conversation going. This can help move the prospect closer to making a purchase.

Creating a winning sales presentation takes time and effort, but it can pay off in a big way. By focusing on the prospect's pain points, highlighting the benefits of your product or service, using visuals and storytelling, providing social proof, and providing a clear call to action, you can create a presentation that resonates with your audience and increases your chances of closing the deal.

# Chapter 7: Negotiating and Closing Deals

Negotiating and closing deals is a crucial aspect of sales mastery. It's the moment where all of your hard work and preparation pays off, and you get to seal the deal. Here are some tips to help you negotiate and close deals like a pro:

1. Set the tone: The tone you set in the beginning of the negotiation can set the stage for the entire process. Be friendly, but assertive, and establish your expectations for the negotiation upfront.

2. Listen carefully: Listen carefully to the prospect's needs, concerns, and objections. This will help you understand their perspective and tailor your proposal to their specific needs.

3. Be flexible: Be flexible and willing to make concessions to reach a mutually beneficial agreement. But be careful not to give away too much or compromise your bottom line.

4. Build rapport: Building rapport and establishing a good working relationship with the prospect can go a long way in the negotiation process. Find common ground and show empathy for their position.

5. Keep the big picture in mind: Remember the big picture and the long-term relationship you are

building with the prospect. Do not sacrifice long-term gains for short-term wins.

6. Know your value: Be confident in the value that your product or service provides and be prepared to articulate that value to the prospect.

7. Address objections: Be prepared to address objections that the prospect may have. Anticipate objections and have answers ready to show how your product or service can overcome those objections.

8. Close with confidence: When it comes time to close the deal, be confident in your proposal and the value it provides. Make a clear, concise ask and provide a simple next step.

9. Follow up: After the deal is closed, follow up with the prospect to ensure that they are satisfied and to maintain the relationship. This can lead to future opportunities and referrals.

10. Practice, practice, practice: Like any other skill, negotiating and closing deals takes practice. The more you do it, the more comfortable and confident you will become.

Negotiating and closing deals can be both exhilarating and nerve-wracking. By setting the tone, listening carefully, being flexible, building rapport, keeping the big picture in mind, knowing your value, addressing objections, closing with confidence, following up, and practicing, you can become a sales hero who closes deals with ease and finesse.

# Chapter 8: Building and Managing a Sales Team

Building and managing a sales team is essential for scaling your sales efforts and achieving long- term success. Here are some tips for building and managing a successful sales team:

1. Define your sales goals and objectives: Before building your sales team, you need to define your sales goals and objectives. These should be specific, measurable, achievable, relevant, and time- bound.

2. Identify the right people: Hire salespeople who have the necessary skills, experience, and personality traits to succeed in your industry and with your product or service.

3. Provide training and development: Invest in the training and development of your sales team. This can include product training, sales training, and ongoing coaching and mentoring.

4. Set clear expectations and KPIs: Set clear expectations and KPIs for your sales team. This will help them stay focused and motivated to achieve their goals.

5. Foster a positive culture: Create a positive and supportive culture within your sales team. This can include team-building activities, recognition and rewards, and open communication.

6. Implement effective sales processes: Implement effective sales processes that enable your sales team to work efficiently and effectively. This can include lead management, pipeline management, and forecasting.

7. Use technology to your advantage: Use technology to streamline your sales processes and give your team

the tools they need to succeed. This can include CRM software, sales automation tools, and data analytics.

8. Monitor performance and adjust as needed: Monitor the performance of your sales team and adjust your strategy as needed. This can involve analyzing data, conducting performance reviews, and making changes to your processes or team, as necessary.

9. Lead by example: Lead by example and demonstrate the behaviors and values that you expect from your sales team. This can include setting an example for work ethic, communication skills, and problem-solving.

10. Continuously improve: Continuously improve your sales team and your sales processes. This involves being open to feedback, learning from your mistakes, and seeking out new opportunities for growth and development.

Building and managing a successful sales team is a challenging and rewarding task. By defining your goals and objectives, hiring the right people, providing training and development, setting clear expectations and KPIs, fostering a positive culture, implementing effective sales processes, using technology to your advantage, monitoring performance, leading by example, and continuously improving, you can build a sales team that can achieve long-term success.

# Chapter 9: Leveraging Technology for Sales Success

Technology has become an essential tool for sales success in the modern world. With so many sales tools and software available, it can be challenging to know which ones to use and how to use them effectively. In this chapter, we will explore some of the most popular and effective ways to leverage technology for sales success.

1. CRM Software: A customer relationship management (CRM) system is a tool that allows you to track and manage your interactions with customers and prospects. It can help you to keep track of leads, manage your sales pipeline, and automate many sales

tasks. CRM software can also help you to analyze your sales data and identify areas for improvement.

2. Sales Automation Tools: Sales automation tools help to streamline your sales processes and reduce the time and effort required to close deals. These tools can automate tasks like email marketing, lead nurturing, and social media outreach. By automating these tasks, you can free up time to focus on more strategic sales activities.

3. Social Media: Social media platforms like LinkedIn, Twitter, and Facebook can be valuable tools for sales professionals. They provide a way to connect with potential customers and engage with them in a more casual and informal setting. Social media can also help you to build your brand and reputation and stay top of mind with your target audience.

4. Data Analytics: Data analytics tools help you to make sense of your sales data and identify trends and patterns. By analyzing your data, you can identify areas for improvement and adjust your sales strategy accordingly. Data analytics can also help you to forecast sales and identify areas of potential growth.

5. Video Conferencing: Video conferencing tools like Zoom and Microsoft Teams have become essential for sales professionals in the wake of the COVID-19 pandemic. They provide a way to connect with customers and prospects virtually and enable remote sales meetings and presentations.

6. Mobile Apps: Mobile apps can help sales professionals to stay connected and productive while on the go. Many CRM systems and sales automation tools have mobile apps that enable sales reps to access their sales data and perform sales tasks from anywhere.

7. Virtual Reality: Virtual reality is an emerging technology that is being used in sales to provide immersive and interactive product demonstrations. Virtual reality can help to provide a more engaging and memorable sales experience for customers and prospects.

Leveraging technology is critical for sales success in the modern world. By using CRM software, sales automation tools, social media, data analytics, video conferencing, mobile apps, and virtual reality, sales professionals can streamline their processes, engage with customers and prospects, analyze their sales data, and provide an immersive and interactive sales experience. As technology continues to evolve, it will become even more critical for sales professionals to stay up to date and adapt their strategies accordingly.

# Chapter 10: Using Social Media for Sales Success

Social media has become an increasingly useful tool for sales professionals looking to connect with potential customers and grow their business. In this chapter, we will explore how sales professionals can use social media to build relationships, establish their brand, and ultimately close more deals.

1. Identify Your Target Audience: Before you begin using social media for sales, it's essential to identify your target audience. Who are the people you're trying to reach? What social media platforms are they most active on? By understanding your target audience, you can tailor your social media strategy to

reach the people who are most likely to be interested in your product or service.

2. Build Your Brand: social media provides an opportunity to establish your brand and showcase your expertise. By sharing valuable content, engaging with your audience, and participating in relevant conversations, you can position yourself as a thought leader in your industry. This can help to build trust with potential customers and establish your credibility as a sales professional.

3. Engage with Your Audience: social media is all about building relationships. It is essential to engage with your audience regularly by responding to comments and messages, sharing content that is relevant to their interests, and participating in group discussions. By building a community of followers, you can keep your brand top of mind and establish yourself as a trusted resource in your industry.

4. Leverage Paid Advertising: While organic reach on social media can be limited, paid advertising can help to expand your reach and target specific audiences. Platforms like Facebook and LinkedIn offer sophisticated targeting options that allow you to reach people based on demographics, interests, and

behaviors. By investing in social media advertising, you can reach a broader audience and drive more leads and sales.

5. Use Social Listening: Social listening is the process of monitoring social media channels for mentions of your brand, competitors, or industry keywords. By listening to what people are saying about your brand and industry, you can identify opportunities to engage with potential customers and address any concerns or issues they may have.

6. Measure Your Results: Like any marketing strategy, it is important to measure your results to see what's working and what's not. Use social media analytics tools to track your engagement, reach, and conversions. By analyzing your results, you can adjust your social media strategy to improve your performance and drive more sales.

Social media has become an essential tool for sales professionals looking to build relationships and establish their brand. By identifying your target audience, building your brand, engaging with your audience, leveraging paid advertising, using social listening, and measuring your results, you can use social media to drive more leads and sales for your business. As social media continues to evolve, it's essential to stay up to date on the latest trends and best practices to stay ahead of the competition.

# Chapter 11: Providing Excellent Customer Service

In the world of sales, providing excellent customer service is crucial for building strong, long-lasting relationships with your customers. In this chapter, we will explore the key elements of providing excellent customer service, and how they can help you to retain customers and grow your business.

1. Be Responsive: One of the most important elements of providing excellent customer service is being responsive. This means responding promptly to customer inquiries, whether it is by phone, email, or social media. When a customer contacts you with a question or concern, they want to know that their needs are taken seriously. By responding quickly and

efficiently, you can demonstrate that you value their business and are committed to providing a high level of service.

2. Listen to Your Customers: Another critical element of excellent customer service is listening to your customers. When a customer contacts you with a question or concern, take the time to listen to what they have to say. Make sure you understand their needs and concerns and do your best to address their issues in a timely and effective manner. By listening to your customers and taking their feedback into account, you can improve your products and services and build stronger relationships with your customers.

3. Be Empathetic: Providing excellent customer service also means being empathetic to your customers' needs and concerns. When a customer contacts you with a problem, try to put yourself in their shoes and understand how they are feeling. By showing empathy and understanding, you can build trust with your customers and demonstrate that you care about their well-being.

4. Offer Solutions: When a customer has a problem, they want to know that you can help them find a solution. Providing excellent customer service means

being initiative-taking and offering solutions to their problems. This might involve troubleshooting issues with a product, offering a refund or exchange, or providing additional support and resources. By going above and beyond to help your customers, you can demonstrate your commitment to their satisfaction and build a strong reputation for your business.

5. Follow Up: After resolving a customer issue, it is important to follow up and ensure that they are satisfied with the outcome. This could involve sending a follow-up email or survey, or reaching out to the customer personally to check in. By following up with your customers, you can demonstrate that you care about their experience and are committed to providing excellent service.

6. Continuously Improve: Finally, providing excellent customer service means continuously improving your products and services based on customer feedback. Use customer feedback to identify areas where you can improve and make changes to your products and services accordingly. By continuously striving to improve, you can show your customers that you are committed to providing the best possible experience and build a loyal customer base.

In conclusion, providing excellent customer service is essential for building strong, long-lasting relationships with your customers. By being responsive, listening to your customers, being empathetic, offering solutions, following up, and continuously improving, you can demonstrate your commitment to customer satisfaction and build a reputation for your business as a provider of excellent service. Remember, the success of your business depends on the satisfaction of your customers, so make sure that providing excellent customer service is a top priority.

# Chapter 12: Measuring and Analyzing Sales Performance

Measuring and analyzing sales performance is a critical part of any successful sales strategy. By tracking your sales metrics and analyzing your performance, you can identify areas for improvement and make data-driven decisions that can help you to achieve your sales goals. In this chapter, we will explore the key elements of measuring and analyzing sales performance, and how you can use these insights to optimize your sales process and drive revenue growth.

1. Key Performance Indicators (KPIs): The first step in measuring and analyzing sales performance is identifying the key performance indicators (KPIs) that matter most to your business. KPIs are metrics that help you track your progress towards your sales goals, and can include metrics such as sales revenue, conversion rates, average deal size, and customer acquisition costs. By tracking these metrics over time, you can gain insights into how your sales process is performing and identify areas for improvement.

2. Sales Funnel Analysis: Another key element of measuring and analyzing sales performance is analyzing your sales funnel. A sales funnel is a visual representation of the steps that a potential customer goes through on their journey towards making a purchase. By tracking the number of leads at each stage of the funnel, you can identify areas where your sales process may be bottlenecked or underperforming and adjust improve your conversion rates and move more leads through the funnel.

3. Sales Forecasting: Sales forecasting is another crucial tool for measuring and analyzing sales performance. By forecasting your sales based on historical data and current trends, you can project your future revenue and identify any gaps or opportunities in your sales pipeline. This can help you to optimize your sales process and ensure that you have the resources and capacity to meet your sales goals.

4. Sales Performance Dashboards: To help you track and analyze your sales performance, it can be useful to create a sales performance dashboard. A sales performance dashboard is a visual representation of your sales data and can include charts and graphs that show your sales metrics and KPIs over time. By regularly reviewing your sales performance dashboard, you can stay on top of your sales data and make data-driven decisions that can help you to achieve your sales goals.

5. Sales Analysis Tools: Finally, there are a variety of sales analysis tools and software solutions available that can help you to measure and analyze your sales performance. These tools can provide detailed insights into your sales data and can help you to

identify patterns and trends that may not be immediately apparent from manual analysis. By leveraging the power of data and technology, you can gain a deeper understanding of your sales process and optimize your sales strategy for maximum effectiveness.

In conclusion, measuring and analyzing sales performance is an essential part of any successful sales strategy. By tracking your sales metrics, analyzing your sales funnel, forecasting your sales, creating sales performance dashboards, and leveraging sales analysis tools, you can gain a deep understanding of your sales process and identify areas for improvement. By using data and insights to optimize your sales strategy, you can drive revenue growth and achieve your sales goals.

# Chapter 13: Continuous Improvement and Growth

Continuous improvement and growth are the key to sustained success in sales. Even the most successful sales professionals and organizations cannot afford to rest on their laurels, as the market is constantly changing, and new challenges and opportunities are always arising. In this chapter, we will explore the key elements of continuous improvement and growth in sales, and how you can use these insights to take your sales performance to the next level.

1. Learning and Development: The first step in continuous improvement and growth is investing in learning and development. By keeping up to date with the latest trends, techniques, and best practices in sales, you can continually refine your skills and stay ahead of the curve. This can involve attending sales training sessions, reading sales books and blogs, and networking with other sales professionals to learn from their experiences and insights.

2. Feedback and Self-Assessment: Another key element of continuous improvement and growth is seeking feedback and conducting self-assessments. By soliciting feedback from your customers, colleagues, and managers, you can gain valuable insights into areas for improvement and identify any blind spots in

your sales process. Self-assessments can also help you to reflect on your strengths and weaknesses as a sales professional and identify areas where you may need to focus your efforts to achieve your sales goals.

3. Experimentation and Innovation: In addition to learning and development and feedback and self-assessment, continuous improvement and growth in sales also involves experimentation and innovation. By trying new techniques and approaches, you can discover new ways to connect with your customers, improve your conversion rates, and drive revenue growth. This can involve testing new messaging, using new sales channels, or exploring new target markets, among other strategies.

4. Collaboration and Teamwork: Continuous improvement and growth in sales also requires collaboration and teamwork. By working closely with your colleagues and sharing best practices and insights, you can create a culture of continuous improvement and foster a sense of shared accountability for sales success. This can involve regular team meetings, cross-functional collaboration, and peer coaching and mentorship.

5. Agility and Adaptability: Finally, continuous improvement and growth in sales also requires agility and adaptability. In an ever-changing market, sales professionals and organizations must be able to quickly pivot and adapt to new challenges and opportunities. This can involve adjusting your sales strategy in response to market trends, experimenting with new sales channels, or adapting your messaging to better connect with your customers.

In conclusion, continuous improvement and growth is the key to sustained success in sales. By investing in learning and development, seeking feedback, and conducting self-assessments, experimenting with new approaches, fostering collaboration and teamwork, and embracing agility and adaptability, you can continually refine your sales process and drive revenue growth. By taking a proactive approach to continuous improvement and growth, you can stay ahead of the curve and achieve your sales goals over the long term.

www.ingramcontent.com/pod-product-compliance
Lightning Source LLC
Chambersburg PA
CBHW071146220526
45467CB00015B/1988